CONTEMPORARY BROADWAY AUDITION WOMEN'S EDITION

15 Songs in Full, Authentic Editions, Plus "16-Bar" Audition Versions

CONTEMPORARY
BROADWAY
AUDITION

To access recorded accompaniments online, visit:
www.halleonard.com/mylibrary

Enter Code
4356-1542-5097-4650

ISBN 978-1-5400-1200-5

HAL•LEONARD®

7777 W. BLUEMOUND RD. P.O. BOX 13819 MILWAUKEE, WI 53213

Visit Hal Leonard Online at
www.halleonard.com

PREFACE

It's become a custom in professional circles, community theatres and even large universities for a "16-bar" version of a song to be required for auditions. This means around 30 seconds of music. But what if they like you and say, "Sing the whole song." This collection of songs has you ready for that situation.

Not only that, it would be crazy to learn a 16-Bar excerpt of a song without learning the whole song first. Only after knowing the entire song very well, and understanding its meaning, as well as the character singing the song, can you possibly succeed in performing an excerpt of a song.

All the songs in this collection are from contemporary musical theatre, dating from 2002 to 2017. Songs were chosen that are particularly good for auditions, coming from a strong character. The excerpt has been carefully selected to show off the voice, with a brief but practical beginning and ending.

It is very, very important for you to practice starting a 16-Bar excerpt over and over. The last thing you want is for the pianist to start and you are not ready, or are not sure where to come in. That's a very bad first impression.

Break a leg!

The Editors

CONTENTS

Pianists on the Full Version Recordings:
[1] Brian Dean   [2] Brendan Fox   [3] Ruben Piirainen   [4] Richard Walters

Pianist on the 16-Bar Version Recordings:
* Brendan Fox   ** Ruben Piirainen   *** Richard Walters

The price of this publication includes access to companion recorded accompaniments online,
for download or streaming, using the unique code found on the title page.
Visit **www.halleonard.com/mylibrary** and enter the access code.

ABOUT THE SHOWS AND SONGS

THE ADDAMS FAMILY (Broadway 2011)
Music and Lyrics by Andrew Lippa

Charles Addams' *The Addams Family* cartoons, which debuted in *The New Yorker* in 1938 and ran periodically until Addams' death in 1988, satirized the ideal American family by depicting a family of gruesomely ghoulish characters who take pleasure in things macabre. The musical revolves around a dinner date at the Addams' house with the family of Wednesday's boyfriend (and soon to be announced fiancé), a "normal" boy named Lucas Beineke. Wackiness ensues as the seemingly incompatible Addams and Beinekes try to get through the evening together. Wednesday sings **"Pulled"** near the beginning of the musical, as she contemplates with both surprise and delight how her love for Lucas is broadening her life experiences, changing her, and pulling her in a new direction.

ANASTASIA (Broadway 2017)
Music by Stephen Flaherty
Lyrics by Lynn Ahrens

Though the musical is based on the 1997 animated film of the same name, 16 additional songs, new characters, new subplots, and a change of setting for the second act make this adaptation of *Anastasia* almost a completely new production. Anya is a young orphaned woman has no memory of her past. She meets two con artists who have a scheme to dress a young woman up as the Grand Duchess Anastasia, who is rumored to have survived a coup that murdered the Russian royal family ten years earlier. The con artists, Dmitry and Vlad, choose Anya because of her resemblance to Anastasia. They begin coaching her on royal etiquette in hopes they can use Anya to extort the only surviving member of the family, the expatriated Dowager Empress, who is living in Paris. In the first act, Anya sings **"In My Dreams"** about the incomplete and fuzzy memories she has from her childhood. Soon, all begin to suspect that Anya actually might be Anastasia. The three are pursued across Russia on the way to Paris by Bolshevik General Gelb bent on carrying out his father's work of exterminating the royal family. Anya sings **"Journey to the Past"** to close the first act as the prospect of finding her identity waits in Paris. After much distrust and questioning, it is finally determined that Anya is the Grand Duchess Anastasia and she is reunited with her grandmother. Anastasia and Dmitry fall in love and return to Russia.

CATCH ME IF YOU CAN (Broadway 2011)
Music by Marc Shaiman
Lyrics by Scott Wittman and Marc Shaiman

The plot of the musical *Catch Me If You Can* closely follows that of the 2002 film of the same name, which was based on con artist Frank Abagnale, Jr.'s 1980 autobiography, also titled *Catch Me If You Can*. The musical tells the slightly embellished story of Frank Jr.'s life in the 1960s, how he grew up in suburban New York and became a successful con man while still in his teens posing as an airline pilot, physician, lawyer, and other professions. During his adventures he falls in love with Brenda Strong, a nurse working at a hospital where Frank has been impersonating a doctor. When Frank finally comes clean to Brenda about his life of lies, Brenda sings **"Fly, Fly Away"** in response, saying that she would never turn on him and that she loves him for who he is. Later she is tricked into betraying him and Frank is finally caught by persistent FBI agent Carl Hanratty. After serving some prison time, Hanratty arranges for Frank to work for the FBI on fraud crimes to serve out the rest of his sentence.

FIRST DATE (Broadway 2013)
Music and Lyrics by Alan Zachary and Michael Weiner

The musical comedy *First Date* follows the story of a blind date between Casey and Aaron. The two have been set up by Casey's sister Lauren, whose husband works with Aaron. The entire musical, without intermission, consists of the dinner date. Impressions are made and change over the course of the evening, and interludes from friends of the two come in to give their opinions on the date and to provide encouragement. Casey is trying to overcome her love of bad boys who are no good for her, while Aaron is struggling to get over his ex, Allison. Casey sings **"Safer"** in the middle of the show, as she thinks about her issues with men, considers her parents' troubled relationship, and contrasts this with the secure family life of her sister Lauren. By the end of the night, Casey and Aaron have helped each other overcome their problems and look forward to their next date.

GHOST THE MUSICAL (London 2011; Broadway 2012)
Music by Dave Stewart and Glen Ballard
Lyrics by Bruce Joel Rubin, Dave Stewart, and Glen Ballard

The 1990 film *Ghost*, starring Patrick Swayze, Demi Moore and Whoopi Goldberg, tells the story of Sam Wheat, a banker, and his girlfriend Molly Jensen, a sculptor, who at the beginning of the musical are moving into an apartment in Brooklyn. Sam loves Molly, but has difficulty saying it, much to Molly's disappointment. While Sam and Molly are walking home together, Sam is killed in an altercation with an armed man. Instead of crossing over to the other side, Sam remains on earth as a ghost, following Molly but unable to speak to her. With the aid of a psychic named Oda Mae, Sam solves the mystery of who was responsible for his death and saves Molly from danger. *Ghost the Musical* follows the same story as the movie. Near the end of Act II, Molly sings **"Nothing Stops Another Day"** as she tries to move on with her life.

HAMILTON (Off-Broadway 2015; Broadway 2015)
Music and Lyrics by Lin-Manuel Miranda

Hamilton combines American history with hip hop, and tells the story of Founding Father Alexander Hamilton's life from the onset of his career until his death. Hamilton meets and marries Eliza Schuyler in 1780. In the second act, Hamilton is caught in an affair and forced to confess it publicly. Eliza, broken-hearted and angry, sings **"Burn"** as she destroys their correspondences, and robs future historians of evidence of redeeming Hamilton's character.

THE LAST FIVE YEARS (Off-Broadway 2002)
Music and Lyrics by Jason Robert Brown

The Off-Broadway musical *The Last Five Years* paired writer Jason Robert Brown and director Daisy Prince together again after their collaboration on the revue *Songs for a New World*. This two-person show chronicles the beginning, middle and deterioration of a relationship between a successful writer and a struggling actress. The show's form is unique. Cathy starts at the end of the relationship, and tells her story backwards, while Jamie starts at the beginning. The only point of intersection is the middle at their engagement. The relationship has taken its toll on Cathy; she is **"Still Hurting"** after the break-up (the show's opening song), wondering about the love and the lies that Jamie gave her. While at a party celebrating the release of Jamie's new book, Cathy sings **"A Part of That."** Near the end of the show, as Cathy's story goes back in time, she sings of her observations about the lives of other young women and hopes for her emerging relationship with Jamie in **"I Can Do Better Than That."**

NATASHA, PIERRE & THE GREAT COMET OF 1812 (Broadway 2016)
Music and Lyrics by Dave Malloy

The musical is based on part five of the second volume of Leo Tolstoy's War and Peace. Countess Natasha is engaged to marry wealthy Prince Andrey, who is away fighting in the Napoleonic Wars. Natasha becomes involved in Moscow society and fails to make a meaningful connection with anyone. Feeling out of place, she sings **"No One Else"** thinking of her betrothed. Later she meets the charming and roguish Prince Anatole, Pierre's brother-in-law, at a decadent ball. They flirt and decide to elope, despite the fact that Anatole is already married, a fact unknown to Natasha. She breaks off her engagement with Prince Andrey. Her cousin Sonya discovers the plan and determines to convince Natasha that running away with Prince Anatole is misguided and will ruin her reputation and cast her out of accepted society in **"Sonya Alone."** Soon, the Prince's marital status is brought to light and Pierre pays him to leave Moscow. Natasha attempts suicide, but survives. Her fiancé returns from fighting unable to forgive Natasha. Pierre comforts Natasha, and then has an epiphany when seeing a comet in the sky.

NEWSIES THE MUSICAL (Broadway 2012)
Music by Alan Menken
Lyrics by Jack Feldman

Newsies the musical was adapted from the 1992 Disney musical film of the same name, which was based on the true story of New York City's 1899 newsboys' strike. Seventeen-year-old Jack Kelly and other paperboys are homeless orphans just scraping by somehow. Jack has just escaped from a terrible home for juvenile delinquents where was incarcerated for stealing. The publisher of the *New York World* raises the cost of newspapers the paperboys have to buy in order to sell them and Jack leads a strike against the paper. He falls for Katherine, a reporter who is covering the strike for a rival paper and who turns out to be daughter of the publisher of the *New York World*. She is wowed by Jack's leadership and sings **"Watch What Happens."** With the support of the governor, Jack strikes a deal with the newspaper that benefits all the newspaper boys, the strike ends, and Jack decides to remain a newsie in New York as he begins a relationship with Katherine.

THOROUGHLY MODERN MILLIE (Broadway 2002)
Music by Jeanine Tesori
Lyrics by Dick Scanlan

Based on the 1967 movie starring Julie Andrews, *Thoroughly Modern Millie*, the stage musical retained only three of the songs from the movie (including the title song), with additional score. It chronicles the life of Millie, a transplanted Kansas girl trying to make it big in New York in the flapper days of 1922. She is anxious and afraid but excited to be in the big city, and definitely decides to stay there, and not return home. She finds a place to live at the Hotel Priscilla for Single Women, which is run by the sinister Mrs. Meers, who actually is running a white slave trade on the side. The madcap plot has many twists and turns, and shows a cheery slice of life in New York during the Jazz age. Millie decides in the end that rather than trying to marry a rich man, it is only love she is interested in with penniless Jimmy. She belts this sentiment high and loud in **"Gimme Gimme."** Jimmy turns out to be a rich heir to a fortune who has been disguising himself as poor to find sincere love.

WAITRESS THE MUSICAL (Broadway 2016)
Music and Lyrics by Sara Bareilles

The musical is an adaptation of the 2007 independent film *Waitress*, which was written and directed by Adrienne Shelly. Waitress Jenna Hunterson is disillusioned, overworked at Joe's Pie Diner, stuck in a small southern town and unhappily married. She wants to leave her husband and open a pie shop, but becomes pregnant, complicated by an affair with a handsome doctor. At her lowest point, while pregnant, she doesn't recognize who she has become, and remembers her former, hopeful self in **"She Used to Be Mine."** In 2015 Sara Bareilles released an album of the songs written for the stage musical. Changes to some of the songs were made subsequent to the album and prior to the Broadway opening.

BURN
from *Hamilton*

Words and Music by Lin-Manuel Miranda

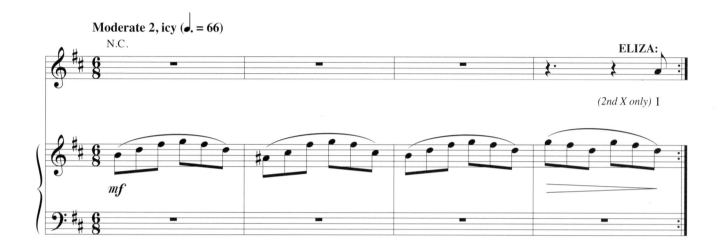

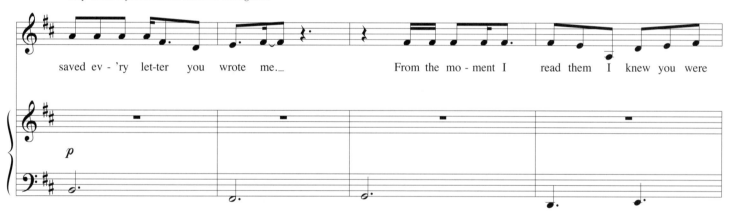

14

BURN
from *Hamilton*
audition excerpt

Words and Music by Lin-Manuel Miranda

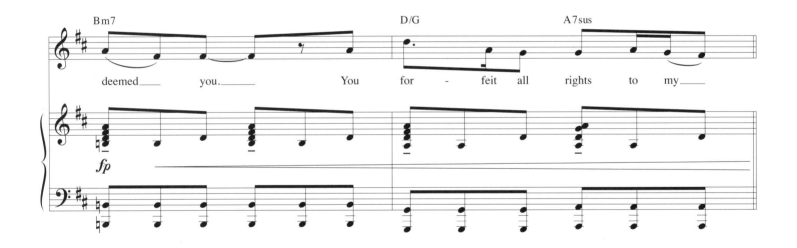

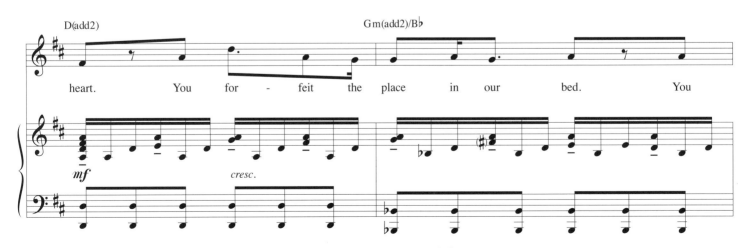

FLY, FLY AWAY

from *Catch Me If You Can*

Lyrics by Scott Wittman and Marc Shaiman
Music by Marc Shaiman

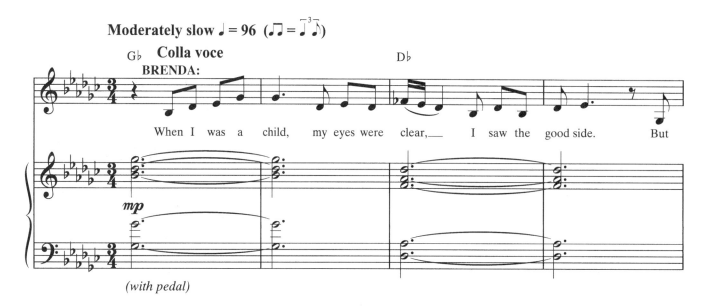

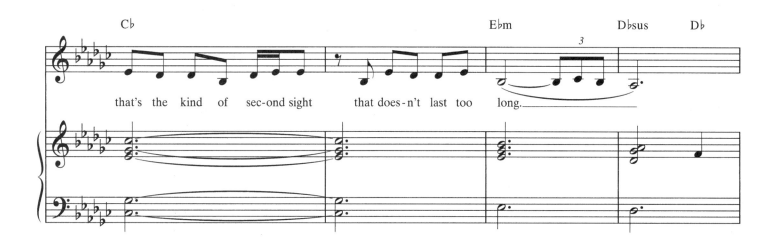

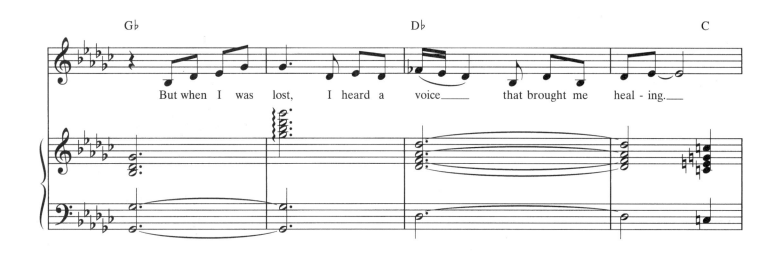

FLY, FLY AWAY

from *Catch Me If You Can*

audition excerpt

Lyrics by Scott Wittman and Marc Shaiman
Music by Marc Shaiman

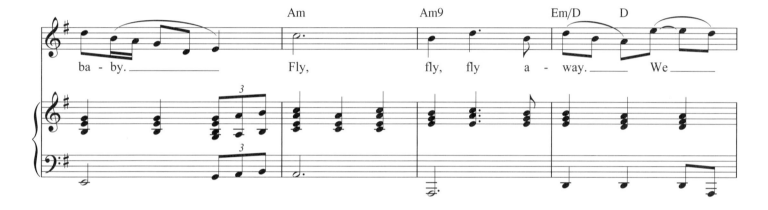

This page has been left blank to facilitate page turns.

GIMME GIMME
from *Thoroughly Modern Millie*

Music by Jeanine Tesori
Lyrics by Dick Scanlan

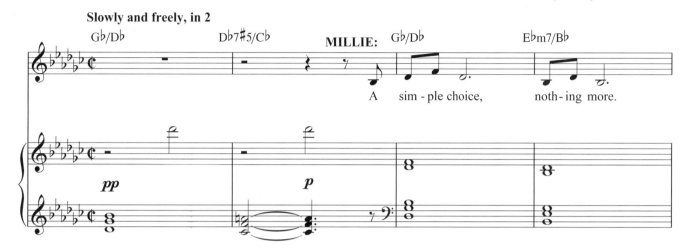

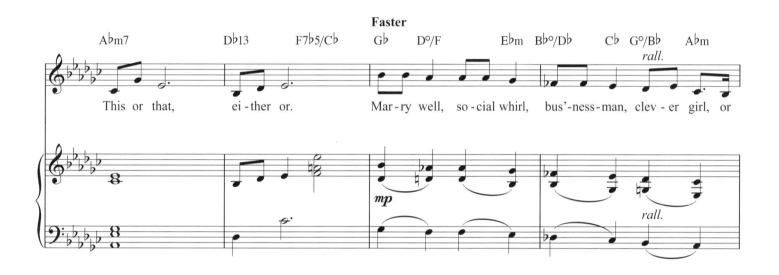

30

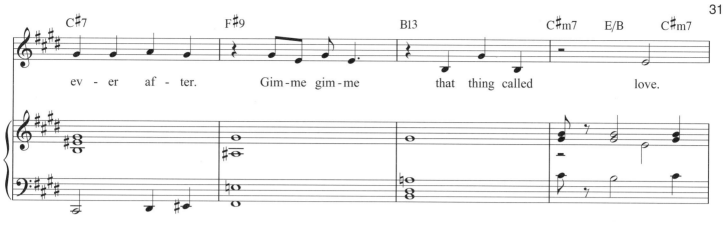

ev - er af - ter. Gim -me gim -me that thing called love.

Moderately, with more confidence

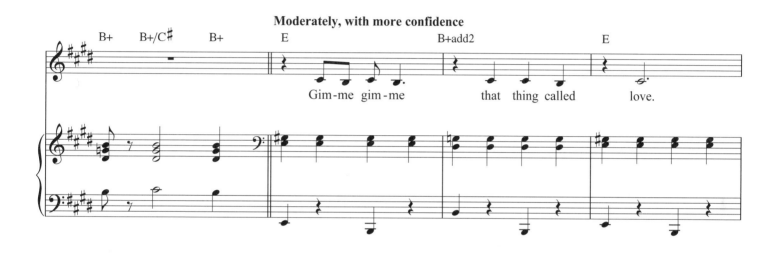

Gim-me gim -me that thing called love.

I crave it. Gim-me gim -me that thing called love.

grad. accel.

grad. accel.

I'll brave _ it. Thick 'n' thin, rich or poor time. Gim-me years and

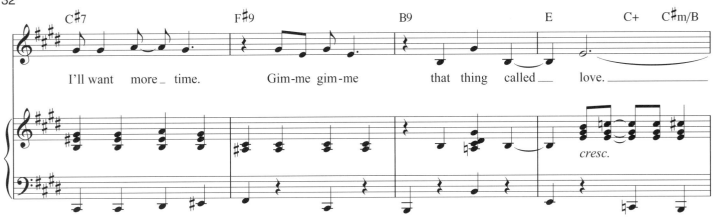

I'll want more time. Gim-me gim-me that thing called love.

Spirited, in 2

Gim-me gim-me that thing called love.

I'm free now. Gim-me gim-me that thing called love.

I see now. Fly, dove! Sing, spar-row! Gim-me Cu-pid's

GIMME GIMME
from *Thoroughly Modern Millie*
audition excerpt

Music by Jeanine Tesori
Lyrics by Dick Scanlan

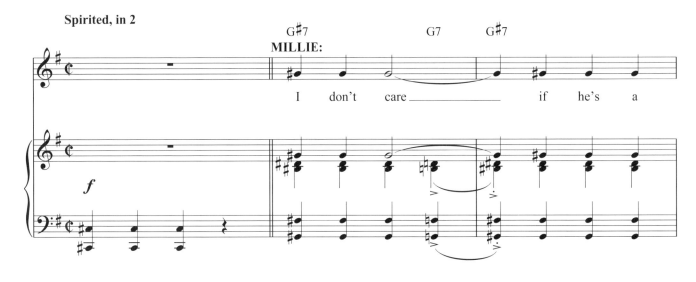

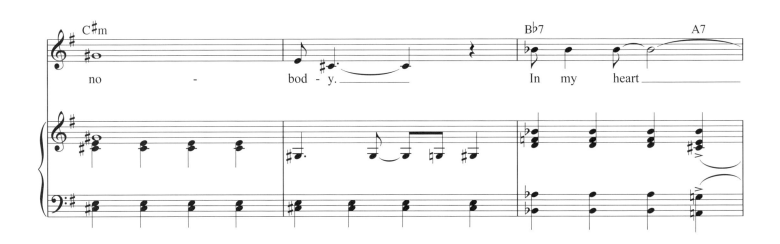

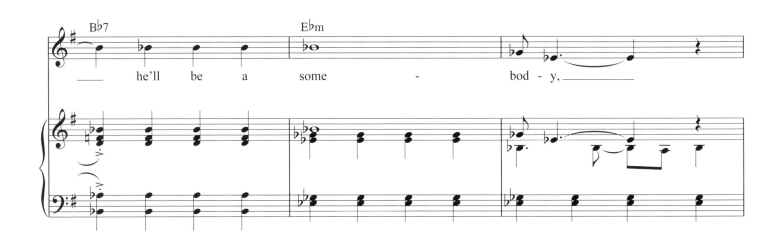

I CAN DO BETTER THAN THAT

from *The Last Five Years*

Music and Lyrics by
Jason Robert Brown

CATHY:
My best friend had a lit-tle sit-u-a-tion at the end of her sen-ior year,

And like a shot, she and Mitch-ell got mar-ried that sum-mer.

I CAN DO BETTER THAN THAT

from *The Last Five Years*

audition excerpt

Music and Lyrics by
Jason Robert Brown

IN MY DREAMS

from *Anastasia*

Lyrics by Lynn Ahrens
Music by Stephen Flaherty

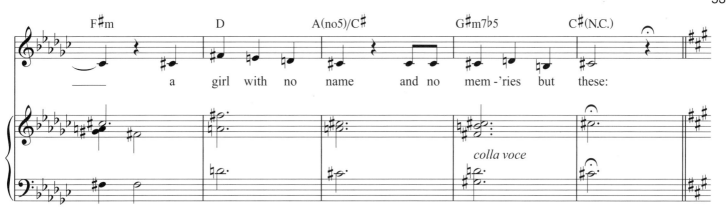

a girl with no name and no mem-'ries but these:

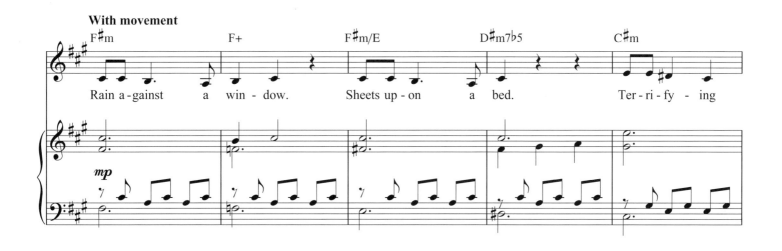

With movement

Rain a-gainst a win-dow. Sheets up-on a bed. Ter-ri-fy - ing

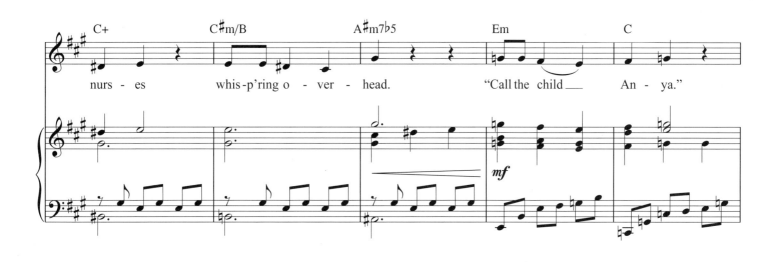

nurs - es whis-p'ring o - ver - head. "Call the child ___ An - ya."

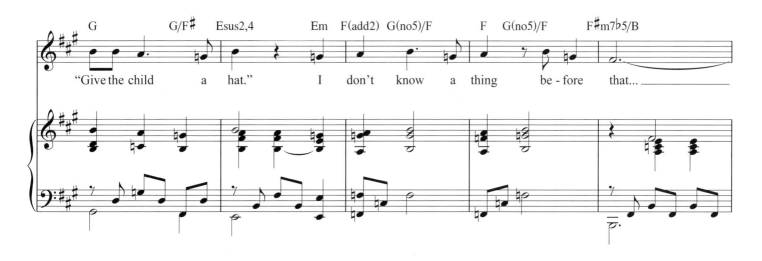

"Give the child a hat." I don't know a thing be-fore that... ___

IN MY DREAMS
from *Anastasia*
audition excerpt

Lyrics by Lynn Ahrens
Music by Stephen Flaherty

This page has been left blank to facilitate page turns.

JOURNEY TO THE PAST

from *Anastasia*

Lyrics by Lynn Ahrens
Music by Stephen Flaherty

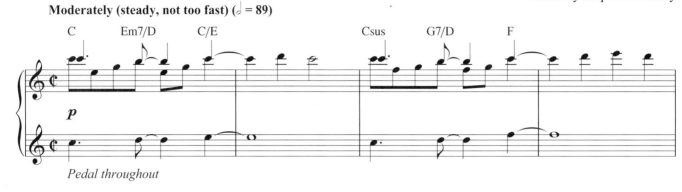

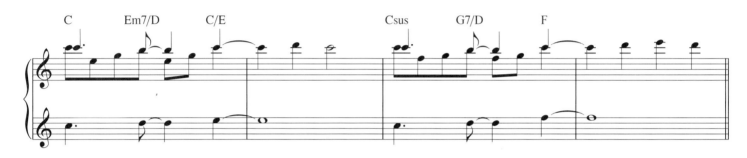

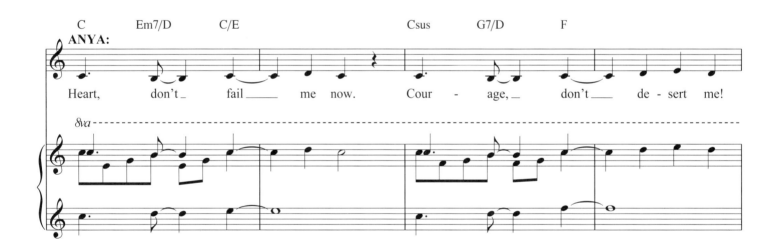

64

69

JOURNEY TO THE PAST

from *Anastasia*

audition excerpt

Lyrics by Lynn Ahrens
Music by Stephen Flaherty

This page has been left blank to facilitate page turns.

NO ONE ELSE

from *Natasha, Pierre & The Great Comet of 1812*

Music and Lyrics by
Dave Malloy
Based on *War and Peace* by Leo Tolstoy

NO ONE ELSE

from *Natasha, Pierre & The Great Comet of 1812*

audition excerpt

Music and Lyrics by
Dave Malloy
Based on *War and Peace* by Leo Tolstoy

NOTHING STOPS ANOTHER DAY

from *Ghost The Musical*

Words and Music by Glen Ballard,
David Allan Stewart and Bruce Joel Rubin

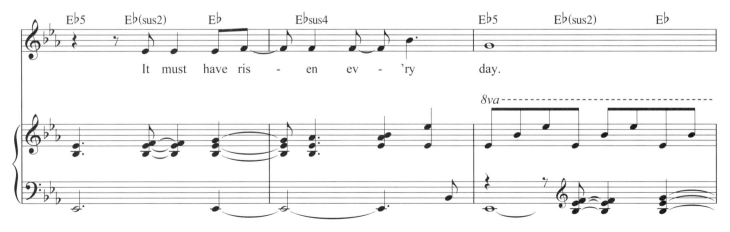

NOTHING STOPS ANOTHER DAY

from *Ghost The Musical*

audition excerpt

Words and Music by Glen Ballard,
David Allan Stewart and Bruce Joel Rubin

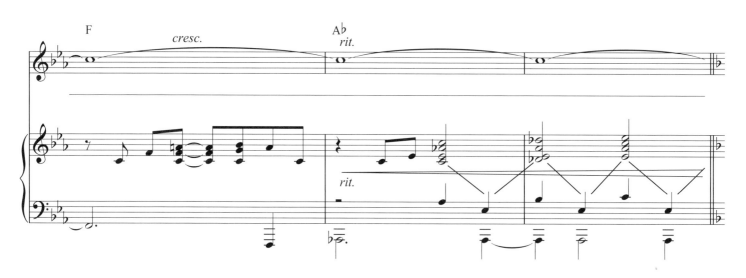

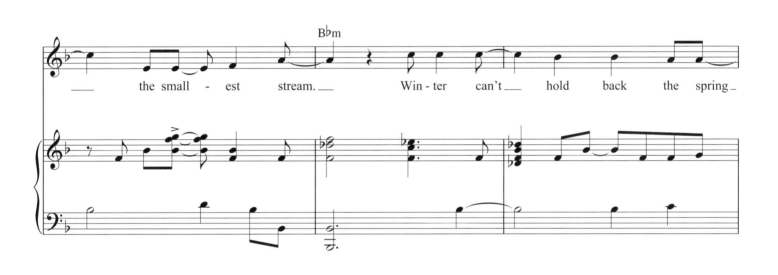

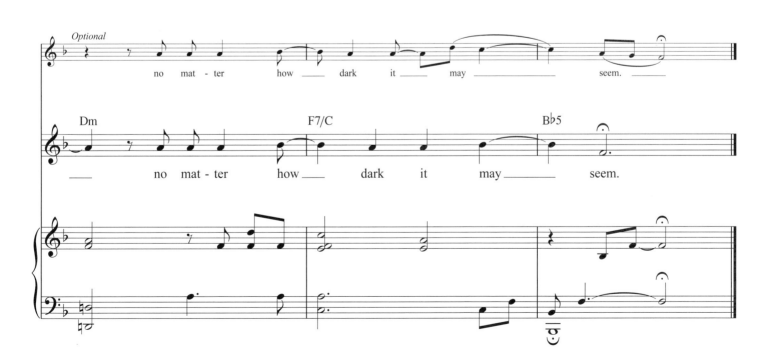

A PART OF THAT

from *The Last Five Years*

Music and Lyrics by
Jason Robert Brown

A PART OF THAT
from *The Last Five Years*
audition excerpt

Music and Lyrics by
Jason Robert Brown

PULLED
from *The Addams Family*

Music and Lyrics by
Andrew Lippa

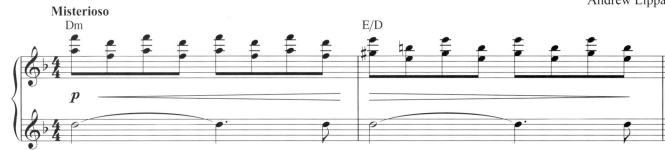

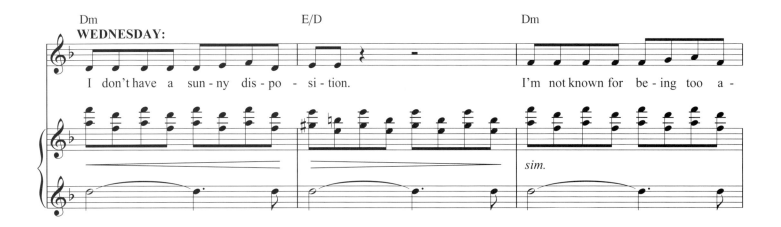

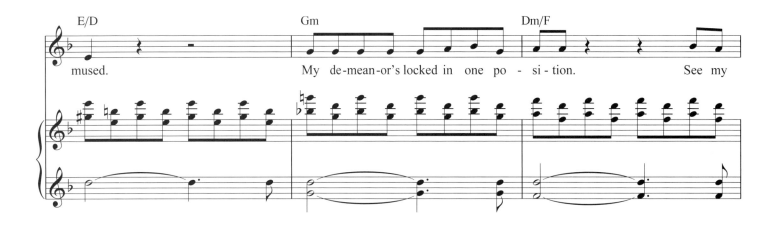

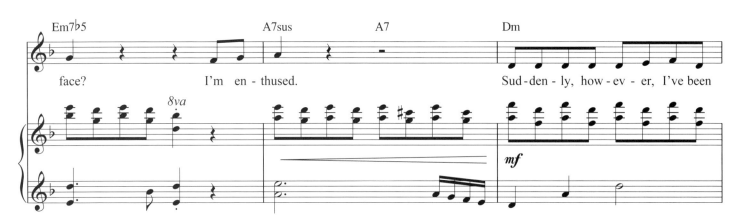

PULLED

from *The Addams Family*

audition excerpt

Music and Lyrics by
Andrew Lippa

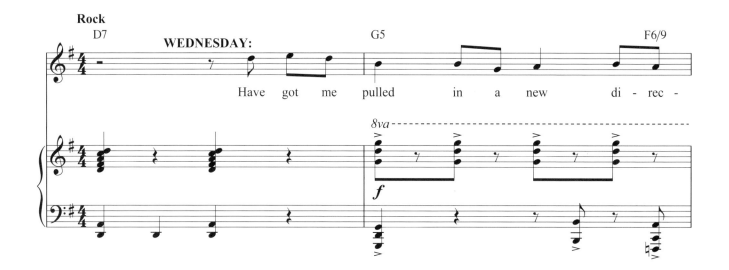

SAFER
from the Musical *First Date*

Music and Lyrics by
Alan Zachary and Michael Weiner

120

SAFER
from the Musical *First Date*
audition excerpt

Music and Lyrics by
Alan Zachary and Michael Weiner

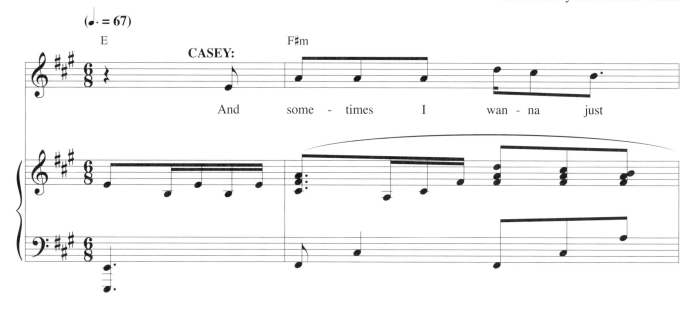

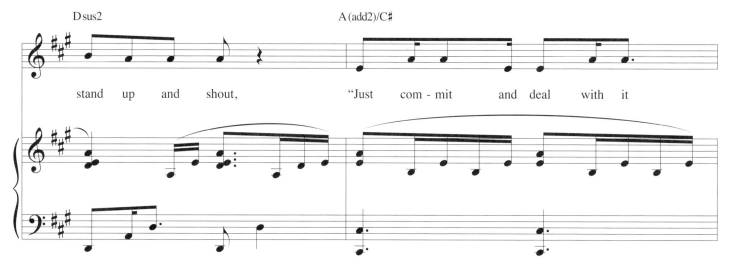

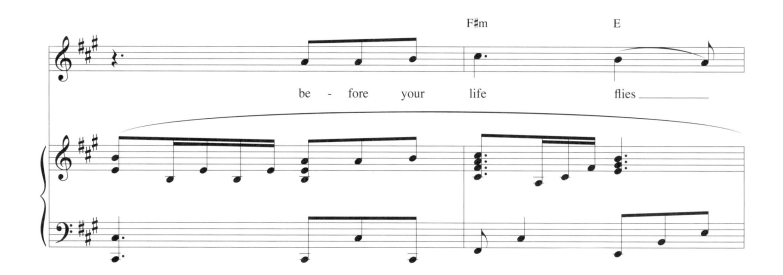

123

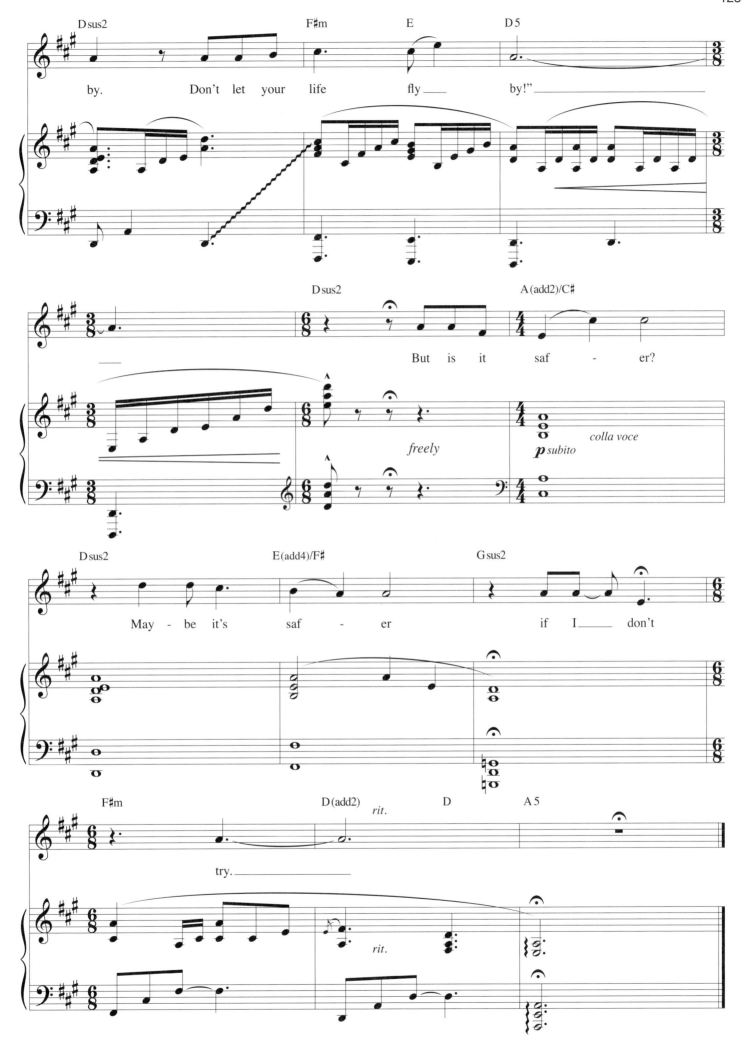

SHE USED TO BE MINE

from *Waitress The Musical*

Words and Music by
Sara Bareilles

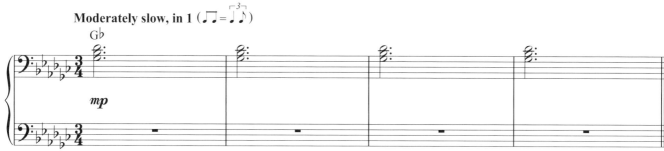

Pedal ad lib. throughout

It's not sim-ple to say ___ that most days ___ I don't rec-og-nize me that these shoes and this a - pron, that place and its pa- - trons have tak-en more ___ than I gave ___ them. ___

She is __ hard __ on her-self. __ She is bro-ken and won't ask for help. __ She __ is mess-y, __ but __ she's kind. She is __ lone-ly __ most of the time. __ She is all of this, __ mixed up and baked in a beau-ti-ful __ pie. __

SHE USED TO BE MINE

from *Waitress The Musical*

audition excerpt

Words and Music by
Sara Bareilles

SONYA ALONE

from *Natasha, Pierre & The Great Comet of 1812*

Music and Lyrics by
Dave Malloy
Based on *War and Peace* by Leo Tolstoy

SONYA ALONE

from *Natasha, Pierre & The Great Comet of 1812*

audition excerpt

Music and Lyrics by
Dave Malloy
Based on *War and Peace* by Leo Tolstoy

Lyrics:

Oh I will stand in the dark for you __
I will hold you back by force __
I will stand __ here right out-side your door
I won't see you dis-graced
I will pro-tect __ your name and your heart __
Be-cause I __ miss __ my friend __

STILL HURTING

from *The Last Five Years*

Music and Lyrics by
Jason Robert Brown

STILL HURTING

from *The Last Five Years*

audition excerpt

Music and Lyrics by
Jason Robert Brown

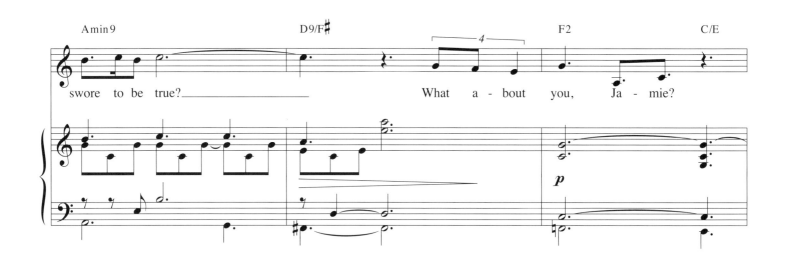

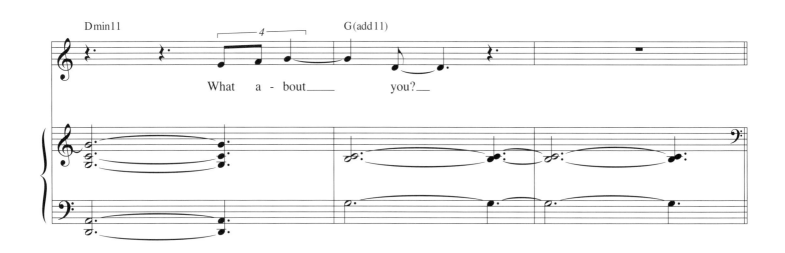

WATCH WHAT HAPPENS

from *Newsies The Musical*

Music by Alan Menken
Lyrics by Jack Feldman

153

WATCH WHAT HAPPENS

from *Newsies The Musical*

audition excerpt

Music by Alan Menken
Lyrics by Jack Feldman

HOW TO USE HAL LEONARD ONLINE AUDIO

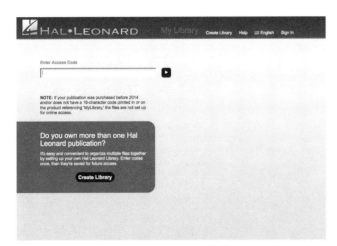

Because of the changing use of media, and the fact that fewer people are using CDs, we have made a shift to companion audio accessible online. In many cases, rather than a book with CD, we now have a book with an access code for online audio, including performances, accompaniments or diction lessons. Each copy of each book has a unique access code. We call this Hal Leonard created system "My Library." It's simple to use.

Go to www.halleonard.com/mylibrary and enter the unique access code found on page one of a relevant book/audio package.

The audio tracks can be streamed or downloaded. If you download the tracks on your computer, you can add the files to a CD or to your digital music library, and use them anywhere without being online. See below for comments about Apple and Android mobile devices.

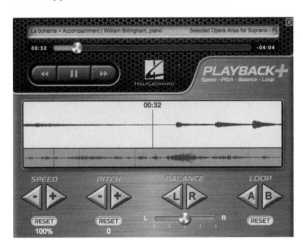

There are some great benefits to the My Library system. *Playback+* is exclusive to Hal Leonard, and when connected to the Internet with this multi-functional audio player you can:

• Change tempo without changing pitch
• Transpose to any key

Optionally, you can create a My Library account, and store all the companion audio you have purchased there. Access your account online at any time, from any device, by logging into your account at www.halleonard.com/mylibrary. Technical help may be found at www.halleonard.com/mylibrary/help/

Apple/iOS

Question: On my iPad and iPhone, the Download links just open another browser tab and play the track. How come this doesn't really download?

Answer: The Safari iOS browser will not allow you to download audio files directly in iTunes or other apps. There are several ways to work around this:

• You can download normally on your desktop computer, saving the files to iTunes. Then, you can sync your iOS device directly to your computer, or sync your iTunes content using an iCloud account.
• There are many third-party apps which allow you to download files from websites into the app's own file manager for easy retrieval and playback.

Android

Files are always downloaded to the same location, which is a folder usually called "Downloads" (this may vary slightly depending on what browser is used (Chrome, Firefox, etc)). Chrome uses a system app called "Downloads" where files can be accessed at any time. Firefox and some other browsers store downloaded files within a "Downloads" folder in the browser itself.

Recently-downloaded files can be accessed from the Notification bar; swiping down will show the downloaded files as a new "card", which you tap on to open. Opening a file depends on what apps are installed on the Android device. Audio files are opened in the device's default audio app. If a file type does not have a default app assigned to it, the Android system alerts the user.